ure
with a Little Bit of Class

Decorating Furniture
with a Little Bit of Class

George Grotz

Doubleday & Company, Inc.
Garden City, New York
1969

Library of Congress Catalog Card Number 69–12854
Copyright © 1969 by George Grotz
ALL RIGHTS RESERVED
Printed in the United States of America
First Edition

Preface: Confessions
of a Furniture Doctor

Or our lying, conniving author
tells the truth at last!

OVER the years now, I've written a lot of books about refinishing furniture in which I've tried to convince people that it was easy to do. Well, of course, I was lying all along. It's hard. And I never do it any more unless I'm downright forced into it. As when my brother-in-law comes to visit us from China, and my wife is embarrassed because all we have around the house is foam rubber on black iron frames. So then my wife says, "Come on, George, show them how you can really do it. Show them I didn't marry a fake."

So then we go out and buy a cheap antique, and I refinish it, and right after he leaves I go out and sell it cheap to some antique dealer I know and want to pump for some more funny stories about the business.

So I've finally decided to come clean and tell all you beloved folks out there in bookland that the only really easy thing to do with junky furniture isn't to refinish it but to paint it up. Or, putting it in fancier language, to decorate it. And over the centuries, people in the junky-furniture trade have figured out a heck of a lot of ways to do this to get out of the work of refinishing.

George Grotz
Durham, N.H., 1968

Contents

Decorating Furniture with a Little Bit of Class

Part I. Finding the Raw Material

What to look for in used-furniture stores
Where to find the cheap antiques
When to use unfinished furniture
Instant furniture kits from lumberyards
Mail-order Colonial-reproduction kits

TO begin with, we make the assumption that you are *not* a nice little old lady to whom "decorating" means painting up tin trays and wastepaper baskets. Not by a long shot. You are—or should be—somebody who wants interesting furniture and can't afford to buy pieces as good as you'd like to have. So here are some places where you can get it from inexpensive to downright cheap—and make it look like something by slapping on one of the decorative ("opaque") finishes that most of this book is about.

(If you *are* a nice little old lady or are planning to be one, you can get all kinds of patterns and supplies for painting flowers and stuff from the following excellent sources: Peg Hall Studios, 111 Clapp Road, Scituate, Massachusetts 02066. Or Jacob and Jane Zook, Paradise, Pennsylvania 17562. Or Marie Mitchell's Découpage Center, 16111 Mack Avenue, Detroit, Michigan 48224.)

1. What to Look for in Used-Furniture Stores

The ones run by charities—at least when the wicked aren't prospering!

MY wife has a way of turning her nose up at anything that looks dirty and crummy. Which I suppose is all right in a wife, since I'd just as soon live in a clean house as any other reformed bachelor. But it makes her a lousy shopper in a used-furniture store. She always ends up in the corner where the manager has put what he considers his priceless antiques. The trouble is that he's so afraid of being taken advantage of by an antique dealer that he has put wildly improbable prices on his high-class junk. (He's being taken advantage of, all right, but I'll tell you later about how the dealers do that.)

Anyway, while my wife is running her lily-white fingertips over the high-gloss varnish some fool has spilled all over the Victorian walnut pieces, I head straight for the kitchen-furniture department. This is the stuff the managers consider too cheap to scrape down and refinish, so they've thrown it on the floor just as it came off the pickup trucks and priced it with chalk between two and ten dollars. In some places you will find tricky

See also Part IV - Pasting things on

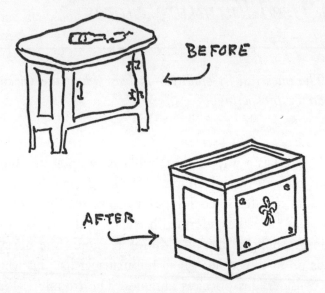

BEFORE

AFTER

The mess at the top left was a kitchen cabinet with an enamel top that cost $4.00 in a used-furniture store. A lumberyard cut a new top and edges to measure and sold us the paste-on fleur-de-lys. I cut off the legs. The piece was then painted a dusty pink, and the decorations were antiqued white. Total time consumed—including the trip to the lumberyard—about five hours.

prices like $2.25 and $7.85, which I assume are supposed to indicate that the marker has some idea of what he's doing.

Now, you aren't going to find any priceless antiques

over here under the three or four layers of paint. But you are going to find among the debris some wooden pieces that are terribly inexpensive raw material for anyone who wants to save money on furnishing a place and who reads the rest of this book. The point is that for decorating furniture you don't have to remove the layers of old paint, but just sand them smooth and cover them with one of the popular opaque finishes.

The most useful things—and therefore the first to go—are shelves. For these, keep in mind that what is before your eyes can *very* easily be modified with a handsaw. It only takes two straight cuts to saw an impossible cabinet off the top or bottom or to shorten a five-shelf piece to four shelves. In the case of cabinets, visualize how much better they might look with their legs sawed off. A crude table can become a different animal altogether if you saw its legs off short enough for a coffee table finished with my imitation mandarin-red lacquer—fast and easy.

Black, gold, pastel, and antiqued finishes can do things to sturdy $1.00 and $2.00 chairs that you wouldn't believe until you came to our house. And don't forget metal porch and garden chairs and tables. These also go cheap, and when the rust is smoothed down and they are sealed with a coat of shellac, they will finish beautifully from a spray can—flat black or aluminum silver will often give a Bauhaus look to them.

Incidentally, I suppose I should make it clear to the innocents out there that the stores I am talking about are used-furniture stores run by charitable organizations.

Being grown-up is harder than it looks at first, and everybody isn't exactly honest out there in the cold, cruel world.

In some cities the Goodwill stores will dominate; in others, the Salvation Army or the St. Vincent de Paul Society. And, of course, many other religious and civic groups handle this sort of thing through annual bazaars or bargain sales. The stores run by the Junior League aren't of much use to us, because the young ladies running them take the good stuff home before anybody else can get it.

Which brings us to the way the managers of even the charity-operated stores sometimes get taken for a ride. I won't say how often this happens, but I know for certain of one such charity-operated store in an Eastern city of some size which has two trucks out every day picking up donations. The fellows driving the trucks pick up the stuff, all right, but before they return to the store, they drive up to the back doors of a couple of antique dealers and give them a first chance to inspect the loot of the day. And there, for a couple of bucks, the really good stuff goes.

Oh, alas and alack, such is the nature of man, and what can we ever do about it? The big fish eat the little fish, and the wicked prosper.

2. Where to Find the Cheap Antiques

Revealing the best sources for Late Victorian and "barn furniture."

I USUALLY put this kind of information only in my $4.95 books, and so today you are getting a break! If you sneakily read this chapter while you're standing around in some bookstore wasting your time *and then don't buy this book*—well, you and I are finished, Buster!

To begin with, let's define our terms. By cheap antiques I mean boxes, trunks, shelves, storage pieces, and tables and chairs that you can buy for, say, under $20 for the larger pieces and for $3.00 to $11 for the smaller pieces and chairs.

Now, these things come in two breeds: the last of the Victorian furniture (almost always heavy oak) and what I call barn furniture. If you've got serendipity— which I don't—both can be stumbled on almost anywhere. But if you are planning a vacation next summer, there are places to go where you can be sure of finding them. Let's start with the Late Victorian.

The craze for antiques has reached the point where anything made out of oak is considered an antique. And all this Late Victorian stuff *was* oak, right up to

1915. This includes office furniture, and though some of it may not look like very much—square and heavy—to my mind it is the best long-term investment anybody could make. In another fifty years it will be considered quaint and called Early American. (If you really want the dope on these things, see the later pages of that invaluable tome *The New Antiques.**)

Where it comes from in any quantity, of course, are the cities where large urban-renewal projects are underway. Right now, this means from the junk shops (and yards) of Boston, New Haven, and especially Providence. Providence not only is being torn down and rebuilt, it is also centrally located in the Northeast and has become a trading center. Junk dealers with stuff to sell often haul it to the Providence area, where there are about thirty antique shops specializing in Victoriana that will take it off their hands cheap—and resell it to the public comparatively cheap, too. You can hardly miss the big old junk stores in Providence, but it is also worth your while to cross the bridge to East Providence. There, the antique shops are spread out on side roads off the highway to Taunton and in Seekonk next-door. Any one of the dealers will give you an association folder showing the location of the rest of the shops in the area. They are smart enough to know that it is good business to push one another's wagons. As a result, dealers come from all over the country to load up their station wagons there.

* George Grotz (Doubleday, 1964), $4.95.

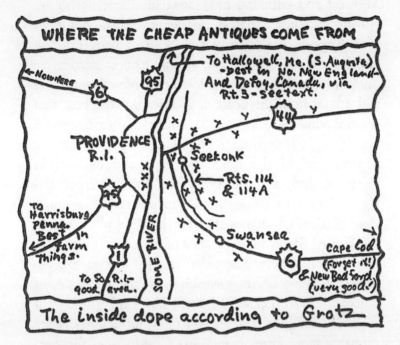

WHERE THE CHEAP ANTIQUES COME FROM

To Hallowell, Me. (S. Augusta) - Best in No. New England - And Defoy, Canada, via Rt. 3 - see text.

← Nowhere

95

6

44

PROVIDENCE R.I.

Seekonk

Rts. 114 & 114A

TO Harrisburg Penna. Best in Farm Things.

95

SOME RIVER

Swansea

Cape Cod (Forget it!) & New Bad ford (very good!)

to So. R.I. - good area.

6

The inside dope according to Grotz

If you are really interested in the lower-priced antiques, you should fork up $4.95 for my book Antiques You Can Decorate With (*Doubleday*, 1966).

What I mean by "barn furniture" is the grain and feed boxes and rustic benches and tables that come from in and around barns and the work sheds of old farms. Just like the Late Victorian furniture, these pieces also come on the market because of social-economic change. In other words, they come from places where small farms are going out of business because they can no longer compete profitably with the big farms of the

Midwest and with the boys down in Florida who are growing tasteless tomatoes in chemical tanks. Southern New England has been picked clean of barn-furniture pieces for years, but you can still find some inexpensive hunks of wood in northern Vermont, New Hampshire, and inland from the coast of Maine. But the best area for this kind of thing in the United States is around Harrisburg, Pennsylvania. The Harrisburg area also has a good deal of the Late Victorian, and once again there are dealers' associations with lists of shops and maps of how to get to them. (Incidentally, the entire state of Pennsylvania is the best hunting place left in the United States for all grades of American antiques.)

Finally, the very best place to find inexpensive antiques is the eastern townships of the Province of Quebec, where the beautiful old farmland spreads out for about a hundred miles east of Montreal. There are probably more farms going out of business in this area than in any place on the continent. And here again a central depot has sprung up, where in the spring and fall the pickers bring in the stuff in a steady stream of small farm trucks. And the dealers from the United States haul it southward from there in a steady stream. I once saw eight trucks there, waiting to load up from the longest barn I've ever seen. Whoever is first in the morning is first in line. But tourists can nose around and buy individual pieces faster—if for a little bit more than the dealers are paying. But not much more.

The depot is the establishment of the brothers Beaudin (René and Leo) in the town of Defoy. Defoy is one of the two towns that make up the "dump," which is just off the new superhighway that connects Montreal and Quebec. The other town is Daveluyville. They lie one on each side of the highway—Defoy on the south, Daveluyville on north—about eighty-five miles out of Montreal. But don't bother looking for them on an American map. You have to wait until you get to Canada to pick one up at a gas station there. It's a long way, but I guarantee it's worth it.

Lately I've been hearing rumors about a dump being set up in the Province of Ontario somewhere between Detroit and Toronto. But the guys who go to these places are pretty close-mouthed about them, and so, if you find it, will you please let me know?

3. When to Use Unfinished Furniture

This is interesting. Maybe you'd better read it.

THERE are only two classes of people who would paint or put *any* opaque finish on a piece of pristine, clean-sanded, unfinished furniture. The first are unmitigated boors who have no appreciation of the beauty of stained and shellacked or varnished wood. The second are discriminating connoisseurs who know exactly what they want and are willing to pay the price and take the trouble to get it. (There is a third class, who don't know what unfinished furniture is and couldn't care less. But they don't concern us in this chapter.)

So let us examine why we discriminating connoisseurs would use unfinished furniture as a base for a decorative (i.e., opaque) finish. There are six reasons:

1. It is not necessary to remove or sand smooth any previous coats of paint.

2. The flat surfaces will be free of dents and the edges clean, sharp, and free of nicks.

3. You can find shelves, cabinets, and boxes in just the size and shape you want for the place you want to put them.

4. If you want to modify the piece, the even-textured and usually soft pine wood can be far more neatly sanded, planed, and sawed than a piece with paint on the surface—which will chip and crack unevenly under cutting tools.

5. You can stain and shellac a piece of unfinished furniture to see how it looks with a clear finish, and if you don't like it, put an opaque finish over the clear one. (Doing the reverse is a lot more work.)

6. It is the perfect base for making a fake antique, if such is your taste, the technique for which is described in my book *Staining and Finishing Unfinished Furniture and Other Naked Woods.**

And so unfinished furniture is ideal for any of the opaque finishes described in this book. It's just that I think you should practice on something cheaper at first. Or at least try staining and shellacking or varnishing that nice wood to bring out the figure and grain. Then, if you don't like the result—or if you get tired of it after a few years—you can put on one of the opaque finishes. For staining and finishing unfinished wood, I would highly recommend the book mentioned above.

*Doubleday, 1968, $1.95.

4. Instant Furniture Kits from Lumberyards

They cut the pieces to length, and you just nail them together.

MY wife says I shouldn't tell you about this, because she thinks it is too hard for anybody except me to do. She thinks I am a genius. Not because I am the world's greatest refinisher and the famous Furniture Doctor but because I can saw a board in half and drive in a

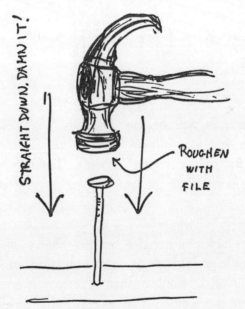

My wife thinks that anybody who can drive a nail in without bending it is some kind of a genius.

nail with a hammer. So please don't tell her there are
other people around who can do these things. And if
you are a poor, frail little thing, there's always some
man around that you can bribe or browbeat into doing
it for you.

Besides, I'm not talking here about hard things to

*Lumberyards will pre-cut furniture kits like this
modern desk, or walls of shelves, out of 1″ by 10″
or 1″ by 12″ "shelving" boards. Then you just
paint them white or stain them cigarette-burn
color.*

make, like tables and chairs, but just shelves and book-
cases, a modern-looking secretary, and low or cocktail
tables. Very few people realize how easy it is to make
shelves and a secretary. The secret is that any lumberyard will cut boards to the exact length you specify
and therefore, in effect, make up an instant furniture

kit for you. And they will sell you a hammer and nails (⌗8, or "eightpenny") to put it together with, in case you don't have them.

To get you started, I am going to tell you the lum-

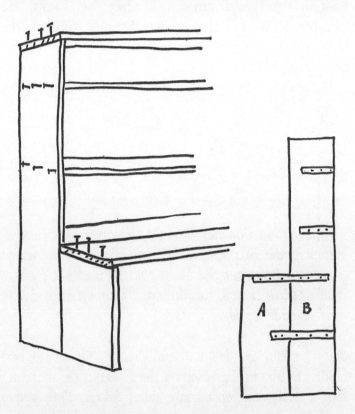

How to put lumberyard furniture together. It takes two people, of course—one to hold the boards while the other nails. With a desk, the sides are put together on the floor first. The cleats hold pieces A and B together and support the ends of the shelves.

ber items of some gorgeous pieces I have made myself. After you have seen how easy it is to nail just one of the pieces together, you will be designing your own like crazy. Don't be afraid to take this book and show the man in the lumberyard which pieces you want. He won't consider you a nuisance, because, quite fairly, he gets to tack a small cutting charge of a dollar or two onto your bill.

Now to the inexpensive and easy-to-assemble tables

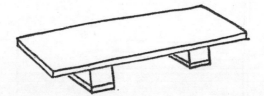

Mass production has brought the price of a flush door under $9.00, and the lumberyard where you get it will pre-cut the boxes that go under it for a small extra charge. Result: a really important coffee or cocktail table.

that you can get from a lumberyard. There are two kinds, and the first is based on the amazing (to me) fact that a flush door costs only about $8.50. This is due partly to mass production and partly to the fact that they are so hollow that it doesn't take much wood to make them. Flush doors come in regular and narrow widths, the latter of which is a fine size for an impressive coffee table if you have a room big enough to take it. The door can be supported on two boxes or on a long, low H of shelving board or plywood pieces.

The second kind of table is based on the fact that, for a slight extra charge, lumberyards will also cut up their basic eight-foot-by-four-foot sheets of three-quarter-inch-thick plywood and pressed board. And you don't have to buy a full sheet, because they have scrap piles of pieces left over from other customers.

Most lumberyards will cut pieces for you only in squares and other rectangles, but if you want a round or free-form top, all you have to do is draw the shape and size you want on a sheet of paper and take it to a millwork shop, where the man will cut your curves on his bandsaw. Lumberyards often have millwork shops next to them; if not, the man at the lumberyard will tell you of one nearby.

The top can be glued to a pair of boxes that you have, or have put together, in order to raise it from the floor. Pressed board is best for these smaller tables, because of the interesting surface and homogeneity of edges, but of course pressed board costs more than plywood. However, there are a lot of things you can do with plywood edges. First, there is a packaged wood-veneer strip sold in lumberyards and hardware stores that you can glue to the edges. Or you can use paper tape, or smooth the edges with spackle—premixed, white plasterlike filler that comes in a can, dries fast, and is easily smoothed with a knife while wet and with sandpaper when dry.

5. Mail-Order Colonial-Reproduction Kits

Fool your friends and confound your enemies with some really great reproductions of Early American furniture that come in kit form.

THE line between an honest reproduction and a convincing fake is a darn thin one—and oh, how I love to cross it! I mean like, man, I've got about as much moral integrity as a Barbary Pirate when it comes to something like this.

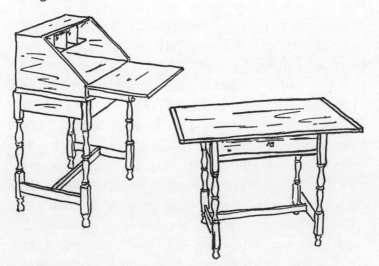

Authentic reproductions of museum pieces like these come in kit form, are inexpensive, and will really amaze your friends and confuse your enemies.

That's why I'm so crazy about the authentic-reproduction kits of Early American furniture put out by Cohasset Colonials of Beverly, Massachusetts. (That's all the address you need, but be sure to enclose a quarter for a catalogue.) The kits range from small tables and chairs to full-sized cupboards, and they are all exact copies of museum pieces, complete with antique-shaped nails.

Now, the proprietor of this business is an honest man and sells his things straight. In fact, I think he might be pretty embarrassed about having an unscrupulous character like me advertising for him. But that's just the way it is, and I guess this country is big enough for both of us.

Anyway, there are two processes discussed in this book that you can reasonably use on these pieces.

The first is stressing and straining and staining a piece to make it look like an antique with the grain of the wood still faintly visible. This is the same process that I describe in *Staining and Finishing Unfinished Furniture and Other Naked Woods*.

The other process is "The Early American Milk-Paint Bit," which I take up in Chapter 7. That chapter is deceiving, but you have to have an audience knowledgeable enough about antiques to know that the really early pieces were painted with mixtures of milk and blood, or milk and colored clays or berry juice, which resulted in fine, soft, dusty reds and blues, and sometimes yellows, with dry color pigment imported from England.

Of course, the reproduction kits aren't cheap, because the workmanship is too fine for that. But once you have a piece put together and finished in *any* way, it's worth about four times what it would cost you in a furniture store. And if you fake-antique it, the value depends only upon how big a liar you are.

Part II. Historical Opaque Finishes

Antique white and other colors
The Early American milk-paint bit
Victorian fake-graining
Early American fake-graining
Gilding chairs and pianos
High gloss on fancy chairs
The limed finish

WHEN it comes to trying to make a silk purse out of a sow's ear, there isn't much that hasn't been tried. And so most of our opaque finishes have a historical background. That's why this chapter is longer than the next one.

On the other hand, all these finishes can be done either in an authentic antique way or with a modern flair. The difference lies in little things, like the way of preparing the surface, "distressing," and colors. But don't get scared just because I'm giving you options. In each case I've kept the process very simple and as stress-free as possible. All tricky-dickey things have been relegated to Part IV. That's for those of you with a neurotic need to prove yourselves.

6. Antique White and Other Colors

The fun finish from France that hardly ever looks dirty.

LOUIS XIV or one of the Louis' started this in France back before the revolution, when everything was decadent and all—at least for all the lords and ladies who were feasting and dancing and doing all sorts of bad things for which they were soon to get their heads chopped off by the peasants, who had been having a really hard time up until then.

For a while there, it was worth your head to get caught dead with an antiqued chair in your house. But times have changed, and now you find them all over—even in the embassies of emerging African nations! Of course, you can use this finish on tables and chests, too, but it is most popular on chairs, because they are small, and this is a pretty showy finish.

A further dividend is that gold leaf seems to be peeking through the high points of any carving on chairs or molding on tables. The effect is that of a piece that seems originally to have been gilded, then painted white, while over a couple of centuries the white paint has worn away from the protruding surfaces and the dust of ages has gathered in the indentations of the carving and molding. I guess the message is that the owner is so rich that he has solid-gold chairs but has modestly painted them white. And now they've been in the family so long that the white paint is wearing off on the high spots and aristocratic grime has collected in the carving and molding.

This, of course, is a lot of malarkey. But it amuses people who don't take their ancestry too seriously. And now, if you would like to try your hand at this little fantasy, here is how you go about it.

First of all, you need a piece with carving on it.

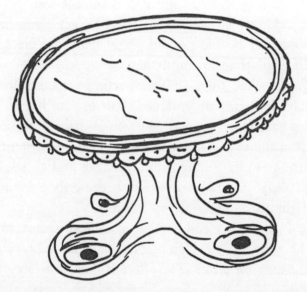

Any piece with carving—especially Grand Rapids reproductions after about twenty years—is a good candidate for antiquing, which when used as a finishing term means painting and glazing.

That's easy to find, because for the last fifty years Grand Rapids has been turning out reproductions of Chippendale and Hepplewhite, as well as the French styles. They all have carvings and moldings and are good candidates for this finish. They are also easy to find, because once the original finish on such chairs and tables becomes worn and cigarette-burned, they land in attics, apartment storage bins, and the $5.00 to $15 bracket of secondhand shops.

What you will need

The finishing materials you will need for a small table (or chair) will follow. (Use your own judgment to increase the quantities for larger pieces such as cupboards and armoires, which, incidentally, are frequently so treated, especially for bedrooms. Also ladies' dressing tables are perfect candidates for this finish.)

1 pint of semigloss enamel
(white, pale green, pink, or blue)

1 tube of raw-umber tinting color

½ pint of indoor or furniture varnish
(*not* "spar" varnish, which is for the outdoors and never dries thoroughly)

2 tablespoonfuls of mineral spirits (the same as paint thinner)
(one to thin the enamel a little, the other to thin the varnish a little)

½ pint of gold paint
(brass color, not bright)

An old washrag or piece of toweling

A cheap two-inch brush

1 quart of paint thinner to clean the wax from the piece (also your hands and brush when done)

The financial or travel section of last Sunday's *Times* to put on the floor

What you have to do

1. Wet the table with mineral spirits and wipe it off. Repeat the process to remove any wax that would cause the paint not to dry well. (I'm using a table as my example, because it includes a large flat surface on top.)

2. Paint the table with the semigloss enamel. (To save time you can use a spray can of enamel or lacquer if you want. Since either of these will give a glossy surface, just rub the table down to a semigloss with ooo-grade steel wool after it is dry.)

3. When the enamel is good and dry, prepare a glaze by pouring the varnish into a soup bowl or coffee tin and adding the tablespoonful of paint thinner and an overflowing tablespoonful of the raw-umber tinting color. Stir well, and brush over the entire piece.

4. Briskly and lightly wipe off the legs with your dry old washrag. You will get the effect of aristocratic grime immediately. If you decide that you have wiped off too much, just brush more glaze on and wipe it off more lightly this time.

5. On the flat top area, wipe the glaze off from the middle, leaving it thicker as you get to the edges. Again, there is nothing critical here, because you can always apply more glaze and wipe it off again.

6. After the glaze is dry, either dry-brush or pad-wipe the gold paint lightly onto the protruding carving and molding or edges of the tabletop. Nothing critical: if you get too much on, just wipe it off with paint thinner and do it again. *Voilà! C'est fini!*

Variations

1. For a more subdued effect, you can dull the white or pastel enamels by tinting them with the raw-umber color. Add a few drops at a time, stir well, and test by brushing a little on a scrap of wood.

2. For a warmer color glaze, tint your varnish with equal parts of raw-umber and burnt-sienna tinting color instead of using the raw umber alone.

3. For a really la-di-dah museum-type antique finish, take a cup of powdered rottenstone (from a paint-supply house—it's cheap) and add enough water to make a paste the consistency of paint or cream. Brush this over the whole surface. After fifteen minutes, wipe

it off, leaving traces in the crevices of the carving and molding.

4. Also see "Gold-leafing" in Part IV for a vermilion under real gold leaf. This is for use on some moldings.

7. The Early American Milk-Paint Bit

What was really used on Colonial paneling and country-made Early American furniture.

BACK when the English were being mean to us—like before 1776 and all that—paint was pretty hard to get. And there were hardly any spray cans at all. So what the local gentry did was save the blood from pig killings and such events and mix it with excess milk from cows. This resulted in a very tough-drying paint that they used on their barns and houses. Almost as good was milk mixed with strongly colored clay or tinted with powdered dry colors imported from England—or local berry juices. There were no strict formulas. People just tried whatever they could think of, and some experiments worked and some didn't. But milk was always the basic ingredient. If you've ever tried to wipe well-dried milk off a baby, you'll see the logic in this. And you might notice that a lot of the new "white" glue is made by Borden's Milk Company.

From a decorative point of view, milk paint is a tough and superflat finish. Also, virtually all Early American furniture and paneling was painted with it. The reproductions of Early American furniture that you see in which the wood is stained and finished with a clear varnish or lacquer may be pretty, but they have no relation to the originals that you can see in Old Sturbridge, Massachusetts.

The famous cabinetmakers of New York City, Boston, and Philadelphia did stain and clear-finish *their* pieces, but they were making English furniture for the very rich in the American Colonies. The simple, functionally designed furniture made outside the cities—which became the classic Early American—was always painted. That most of the original pieces of the era have been scraped down and varnished is a sad thing; it has cut their value to a fraction of what it would be if the original finish had remained.

Now, there are two ways of attaining this finish. The first is to mix yourself some milk paint, and the second is to use any flat water-mix paint and color it with tubes of tinting color to get a shade equivalent to one of the basic Early American colors. Frankly, my sympathies lie entirely with those who choose the first course, because anything that comes out of being really involved in what you're doing can't be bad and may be great. This is how to mix milk paint:

What you will need for 1 quart of milk paint

Powdered milk to make 4 quarts of milk

1 pint of liquid "white glue"

Powdered colors from a large paint-supply company

1 quart of water

What you have to do

1. Mix the powdered milk and glue in warm water.
2. Add colors to taste (universal tinting colors may also be used).
3. Brush it on and let it dry.

Variations

This superflat finish will be ultrasensitive to spotting from grease or oil, and so, while it was usually left natural on paneling, pieces that came into common use were then brushed over with a coat of one part of linseed oil and one part of turpentine or paint thinner. This was left soaking for half an hour and then was rubbed off hard and completely with soft rags. It looks great this way.

8. Victorian Fake-Graining

This is supposed to be a lost art, but maybe you can revive it.

THE basic idea of fake-graining was to coat pine or any other common wood with a tan base coat and then swish a brown glaze over the top with sponges, combs, raggedy brushes, and the like to make it look like some other kind of wood. Just what other kind of wood the Victorian decorators were trying for is hard to figure out. At least I never could. To me it looks just like tan paint with a brown glaze squiggled and squished and combed all over it.

There are exceptions. Some factories turned out pieces done with a very fine and careful touch. Colored borders were put on tops and drawer fronts, and in the middle somebody painted sheaves of wheat and rolling fields and such. Because most such pieces were later painted over or scraped down for the pine to show, the unspoiled items will absolutely skyrocket on the antique market in the next ten years. They are already worth more than those that have been scraped down and finished in the natural pine.

I really can't give detailed directions for fake-graining. You would have to get a piece and copy it. Besides, you have to be a pretty experienced operator with camel's-hair brushes to paint the little pictures. If you're that good, you know as well as I do, if not better, what materials to use. However, I might as well mention that you will need these materials: 1. any flat tan paint for the undercoat; 2. the same kind of varnish-base glaze that I give directions for making in Chapter 6, "Antique White and Other Colors"; 3. for the painted decorations, regular artist's oil colors thinned with Japan dryer for quick drying. At least that's what the original decorators did.

I'm going to discuss some modern opaque finishes in Part III, "What to Do With Unfinished Furniture."

9. Early American Fake-Graining

The worse you do it, the better it looks!

NOW, here is something impressive in the line of fake-graining that anybody can do with really great results the first time out. That's because this kind of fake-graining is *supposed* to look crude as if you had never held a brush in your hand before.

This finish goes back to the early 1700s, when country people either had to make their own furniture or have it made by the town carpenter in his spare time. The commonest pieces surviving today are tables and lift-top blanket chests, with maybe a drawer in the bottom. (Probably a lot more chairs were made, but almost all these were worn out or broken.)

These things are called "primitive" furniture, and they were always strong, crude, functional—and beautiful! Objects designed purely for function always are beautiful. They were also at the roots of the classical furniture style that we call Early American.

The originals were never stained or given a clear finish, or both, as reproductions are today. They were painted with dark-red milk paint—a mixture of equal

Fake-graining Early American style consisted of streaking black paint over dark-red paint made with milk and blood. The work was so sloppy that anybody can duplicate the effect for a classy and amusing piece.

parts of milk and blood. The blood came from a recent butchering. Then, in a charmingly naïve effort to fancy the thing up, somebody would sponge or streak the surface with black paint (made of blood plus soot) in crude imitation of wood grain or in circles or wavy lines just for decoration.

What you will need

Dark-red flat paint—a sort of "barn red"
(You can get something close to this color in a paint store that mixes gallons of wall paint to the color its customers want.)

½ pint of flat black paint

1 pint of boiled linseed oil with ¼ pint of mineral spirits or turpentine added

A brush and a sponge or piece of burlap

Soft cloths

What you have to do

1. Paint the piece red and let it dry.
2. Decorate with the black paint, using the brush without much paint on it (dry-brushing) for streaks, or punching the surface with the brush. Or apply the black paint with the sponge or burlap.
3. When both red and black paint are thoroughly dry, paint the piece with the thinned linseed oil, and after half an hour wipe it dry with soft cloths.

Variation

The black paint can be applied before the red has dried—in fact quite soon—so that the colors blend at the edges of the black streaks.

The wild-looking effect will really fool people, because the worse you are at decoration the more authentic the thing will look.

10. Gilding Chairs and Pianos

A glazed dull gold that fits in with anything and is easy to slop on.

GILDING is another of those decadent French finishes, as antique white is, but it so obviously isn't *supposed* to match anything else that it fits in anywhere in a quiet campy way. If you don't want something quietly campy in your house, you don't love Tiny Tim, and I don't love you.

Also, gilding is the best cover-up finish in the world. Even if the piece is coated with six layers of drippy, sagged, chipped, peeled, and blistered paint, this all becomes "interesting texture" under a coat of dull-bronze gold paint, with or without a brown or green or greenish-brown glaze wiped off in the manner described in the chapter on antique white.

What you will need

1 pint of dark-bronze gold paint, which you will probably have to buy in an art-supply store. (The common bright gold that they used to use on radia-

tors just doesn't make it these days.) This is enough for a piano, because gold paints cover well even in the thinnest coats.

1 pint of satin varnish

1 pint of mineral spirits—to thin both the gold paint and varnish if necessary

1 tube of universal tinting color—dark green or raw umber

What you have to do

1. Clean the surface with mineral spirits, ammonia, or Spic 'n' Span. Let it dry well.

2. Brush on the paint in a nice thin coat, and let it dry overnight.

3. Mix one or two tablespoonfuls of tinting color in varnish, and thin it with two tablespoonfuls of mineral spirits. Brush it on and wipe it off according to the directions given in Chapter 6 for glazing antique white and other colors. Dust of ages can also be applied.

11. High Gloss on Fancy Chairs

A little something special for my lady's boudoir.

HERE'S an easy way to get the high-gloss surface called a French polish. This is a real attention-getter on an occasional or lady's chair—the latter was a very popular boudoir item of the Victorian era. Also called a slipper chair, for reasons that must be obvious to even the meanest intelligence.

This finish is an over-coat finish that can be applied to a chair that has been either finished in natural or stained wood or painted black or rose or gold. It consists of shellac rubbed on in rapid strokes with a pad wet with linseed oil. This brings the shellac—which sticks to the chair, not to the oily pad—to a mirrorlike surface. In olden days, when things were done by hand, pianos were finished this way. But applying this finish to large flat surfaces takes a lot of experience and even more hard work. So let's consider a chair, and if you want to graduate to pianos after that, you are on your own.

What you will need

1 pint of shellac

1 pad of ooo-grade steel wool

½ pint of boiled linseed oil

1 sheet of fine production paper

What you have to do

1. Clean the old surface of the chair with mineral spirits, ammonia, or detergent to remove wax or oil.

2. Sand rough spots smooth with fine production paper.

3. Stain or paint the chair any color your little old heart desires. Dark walnut shows conservative, dignified restraint. Black is spooky. Gold is theatrical. Pastel colors are feminine.

4. After the paint has dried at least twenty-four hours, rub the chair down with the steel wool.

5. Apply a coat of shellac straight from the can without thinning—*but not the can it came in. Always pour paint or stain or other finish into a bowl or can and take it from there.*

6. After the shellac coat has dried overnight, we get down to the fun part. From old sheeting prepare a pad

Always pour any paint or finish into a clean bowl or can before dipping your brush into it. It is the only way to keep your paint or other finish really clean.

about as big as the palm of your hand, or a little smaller, not any larger, with about twelve layers of thick cloth. Wet this with the boiled linseed oil and wipe a thin film of oil over the whole chair.

7. Believe it or not, what you do now is pour a quarter of a teaspoonful of the shellac onto the squeezed-dry

pad, spread it around a little with your finger, and start rubbing it onto one of the risers or rungs of the chair. Start anywhere. For every rung or equivalent area, add a few more drops of shellac. Rub briskly and firmly without stopping while the pad is on the surface; if you don't keep rubbing, the pad will stick and make a mark that is a bother to have to rub out.

This job does take considerable rubbing, say about a minute for a rub, and if a section isn't getting glossy fast enough to suit you, keep adding shellac to your pad a little at a time.

8. After the whole chair is glossy, wipe off the linseed oil with soft rags or, even better, with face tissues. Let the chair dry a couple of days and apply lemon oil or white cream furniture polish.

12. The Limed Finish

A subtle, rich-looking finish for open-pored woods.

FOR a change, this finish comes from England. But it was probably introduced there by the French after 1066.

Anyway, the point of this finish is that the wood is stained or painted one color and the pores are filled with white. Naturally this works best with oak or chestnut, but it can also be done with mahogany or walnut when the wood has been sawed to leave an open grain.

On an old piece, the only way to find out if the wood

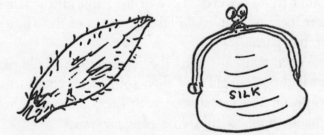

That's a sow's ear on the left and a silk purse on the right, which is what this book is all about— making the purse out of the ear.

has open pores is to strip it with paint remover and a fine-wire or plastic-bristle brush. That will pull out any filler that was put into the pores at the factory before a final finish was applied. When that has been done, you have a perfect candidate for a limed finish.

The trick is simple. Having removed all the filler from the pores, you can leave the wood its natural color and just shellac it. Or you can stain it first, and then shellac it. Or you can apply a thin coat of enamel. Dark green and gray are good. Or a real dark red. Just brush it on hard and thin so that the paint doesn't fill up the pores.

When the base coat is dry, brush flat white paint of any kind onto the surface and scrub it into the pores. Don't use any more paint on your brush than you need to get it into the pores. Do this in an area of about two square feet and immediately wipe the white paint off the surface with a dry pad of folded-over sheeting. Don't try to get every trace of the paint off the flat surface, because you would take too much of the white out of the pores.

When you have filled the pores on the whole piece, let it dry overnight and then softly scuff the traces of white off the flat surface with oooo-grade steel wool. Finally, apply a thin coat of spray wax.

Part III. What to Do With Unfinished Furniture

Preparing the naked woods
Chinese lacquer—the red and the black
The Mediterranean look
Instant antiques

UNFINISHED furniture costs more than the junk you can pick up in secondhand stores, but because of its crisp, clean lines, it is far better for getting a modern look. It is also the only furniture to which you can give a plain or fancy staining job—say from corny maple to imitation teak or rosewood. For the intimate details of that sort of thing, see *Staining and Finishing Unfinished Furniture and Other Naked Woods.** In the following chapters we are mainly concerned with opaque finishes for naked wood. But since a foolish consistency is still the hobgoblin of small minds, I'm going to throw in a little bit about staining, too. Besides, I don't want you to think I'm a cheapskate.

* George Grotz (Doubleday, 1968), $1.95.

13. Preparing the Naked Woods

This is very educational—don't skip it.

I KNOW this sounds like a real drag, but if a beginning is to be made at all, that is where the most care must be taken. The roots of our failures lie not in our stars but in starting out sloppy. Once you start out with a rough or dusty or greasy surface, there is no way of going back, and all your tears won't wipe out a brush stroke of it.

Now, a piece of unfinished furniture *looks* as if it is all ready for you to pounce on it, but it isn't. It's been sanded smooth, all right, but nobody has really dusted it, and all the edges are still machine-worked sharp. The trouble with the dust, of course, is that it will rise to the surface of any finish or paint you put on. And nice as those clean, sharp edges may look, they are treacherous. That is because if they are finished as is, they will dent easily at the slightest contact.

So here are three simple steps to get a perfect foundation for the finish you'll love to touch:

1. Unfinished furniture varies a great deal. In some, the surface is only planed smooth, with the result that when you look across the surface into the light, you will see definite ridges. In this case you are going to have to sand it evenly—it's not hard—with fine-grade produc-

tion paper wrapped around a small piece of flat wood that is easy to grasp with your hand. Rub with the grain until the whole surface has been evenly abraded.

2. Now "cut" or "take the curse off" the sharp edges by rubbing them with *fine-grade* production paper.

3. Any piece of unfinished furniture will still have a little wood dust on it—even if you don't have to sand it. Brushing and blowing this off will work to some extent, but it is much better to wipe the piece off with a damp rag—not a wet rag, because that would raise the grain of the wood, and you'd have to sand it down again.

4. Now is the time to stain the wood if you are going to. But whether you stain it or not, the wood now needs a sealer coat of shellac. The purpose is to stop the wood from being porous—and especially from being more porous in one place than another. The shellac stabilizes the base. You apply with a brush one coat of shellac mixed 50–50 with denatured alcohol. This will also bring to the surface the slightest speck of dust and will make the surface brittle enough so that you can now supersmooth it by rubbing it down—really polishing it—with ooo-grade steel wool.

5. Now give the piece another dusting and wipe it down again with a damp rag.

(In case you have stained the wood in preparation for applying a clear finish, you apply the thinned coat of shellac over the stain, rub it down with steel wool, dust it, and wipe it. Then you are ready for your clear finish—varnish, spray-can lacquer, or what have you.)

14. Chinese Lacquer—
the Red and the Black

For stunning effects that are easier to achieve than it sounds.

HERE'S a finish that can look as modern as tomorrow in Scandinavia while in the background you can still hear the temple gongs booming in Old Cathay. It looks especially good on a small chest of drawers, which you can use in any room of your house, or in a one-room apartment, next to your stainless-steel chair with the black-leather seat and back. You know, sophisticated.

The best color combinations are solid black with dark-gold knobs—or dark red with black knobs. In either case, gold carriage striping can be used if you want to make it look more Chinese, but I prefer the plain, sleek modern look.

Because simplicity and smoothness are the keys to the effectiveness of this finish, you really need the perfect new surface that you get with a piece of unfinished furniture. Besides small chests, record cabinets with one or two doors are also good pieces to do this way. But keep to unfinished wood. Pieces that you have stripped down, or painted ones that you think you have sanded smooth, just never are smooth enough.

What you will need

4 sheets each of fine, medium, and coarse *production paper*. This costs about fifteen cents a sheet but works much faster and lasts longer than old-fashioned sandpaper. It is available at any good hardware store.

1 pint of shellac thinned down with a ½ pint of denatured alcohol

6 pads of ooo-grade steel wool, two of ooooo

1 pint of black enamel or 1 pint of red enamel into which you have stirred well a teaspoonful of black universal tinting color

2 level tablespoonfuls of mineral spirits, with which you thin either of the pints of paint (above) for smoother brushing

Lemon oil or oil-base white cream furniture polish

What you have to do

1. The first step is to round the edges of the whole piece of unfinished furniture you have chosen. This means *all* edges—drawer and door edges, inside and out; top edges and bottom edges. You can start rounding with a small hand plane or with the coarse production

REST
ON
NAIL
HEAD DOWN
(POINT UP!)

Top just painted

To get a good paint job, never paint a vertical surface. To do the front of a cabinet, put the piece on its back as above. Let the surface set for half an hour, and then turn the same way to do the sides. Resting on nail points prevents smearing at edges of the top.

paper. Move next to the medium paper, and then the fine, so that you have a smooth, scratch-free surface. This isn't hard work, but it is time-consuming, and you won't knock it off in an evening; absolute smoothness of the wood is the basis for what the finish will look like in the end.

2. Now brush on the shellac until it stops sinking into the wood, but wipe off any excess with a soft rag before it can dry.

3. After the shellac has dried for an hour or more in a warm room, sand the whole piece carefully but

lightly with the finest grade of sandpaper. After the whole surface has been scuffed, go over it again with a half pad of the ooo-grade steel wool. Finally, blow, brush, and wipe off the dust. When it looks perfectly dust-free, go over it again with a water-dampened rag.

4. Give the piece another coat of shellac, and then sand, steel-wool, and wipe it the same way all over again. (I told you this wasn't a short job—it should take about four evenings.)

5. You now have a fit foundation for the enamel, and the problem comes of getting it on without drips or curtains. The secret of that is to work only on horizontal surfaces, which you achieve by putting the piece on its back and alternately on each side. As you lower the piece to the floor, let it rest on an upturned nail to keep the painted surface off the floor. Let each surface dry in its horizontal position for half an hour before turning it. The illustration shows how to do this without messing it up.

6. After the enamel has dried for two days in a warm room, polish it with the ooooo-grade steel wool, apply the oil-base white cream polish or lemon oil freely with a pad of soft cloth, and rub it in hard for about a minute per square foot. Wipe off the excess oil, and there you are. It's a beauty.

15. The Mediterranean Look

Take a tip from the rich, and stain your furniture cigarette-burn color.

I SEE by the papers that the newest thing in store-bought furniture is the Mediterranean Look. Of course, I've been familiar with it for a long time, because being a Furniture Doctor gets you into a lot of rich people's houses. Through the back door, of course, but you're in.

Now, the Mediterranean is a pretty big lake, with a lot of countries around it. This is very handy for the furniture manufacturers. They can slap the label "Mediterranean" on just about anything they turn out that looks vaguely Spanish, French, Italian, Yugoslavian, Greek, Jewish, Egyptian, Abyssinian, Moorish, or one of the other nationalities that escape my memory. All they have to do is slap a coat of creosote-colored stain on it—and it's Mediterranean. They also use cheap wood and boards that don't match very well, because who can see what's going on under that almost-black stain?

So the furniture manufacturers win all around. But so do you. Nobody will notice the cigarette burns on something that is already the color of a cigarette burn. That's why the rich from Long Island to Palm Beach

The Mediterranean look is great, because what it boils down to is staining your furniture cigarette-burn color.

to Acapulco turned to this finish long ago. All rich people are preoccupied with saving money. It's an occupational disease. (Of course, I mean the really rich— the kind that pay public-relations companies to keep their names *out* of the papers.)

Duplicating this finish is easy. If you live in Mexico or South America, just go down to the local paint-and-hardware store. (It's Señor Cohen's in San Miguel de Allende.) They have only one color of stain, a well-distilled creosote. This has the added attraction of worm- and termite-proofing the furniture. That's also important to the really rich, and a nice talking point for you.

If you live in some silly place like New York City or Playboy, Illinois, or Washington, D.C., just ask for a dark-walnut stain and apply one or two coats of whatever you get. In Washington there's a lumberyard at Seventh and V streets where they sell it in spray cans; these make the job a real snap.

If you are out in the sticks where everybody buys his furniture from Sears, Roebuck & Co., or Montgomery Ward, you probably won't be able to buy wood stain. But at least there will be a paint store, and you can easily mix up a stain by adding *color ground in oil or universal tinting colors* to mineral spirits or turpentine. The proportions to begin with are these:

1 pint of mineral spirits

1 tube of raw umber

1 tube of burnt umber

1 tablespoonful of black

The recipe can be varied to taste. Just be sure to read Chapter 13, "Preparing the Naked Woods," a few pages back, before you plunge in. Remember, you aren't rich. You wouldn't be here with me if you were.

16. Instant Antiques

I can do this in two hours. You should take about two evenings. Which is still a pretty quick trip back to two hundred years ago.

I SEE from the ladies' magazines that heirlooms are all the rage these days. Well, that's all right with me. I'm just a little worried about where the ladies are going to get them. On account of the way the population expands and all, I'm afraid there won't be enough to go around. So I'm going to let you in on a little secret that has kept many an interior decorator and antique dealer in business for years: antiques are skin deep. And you are just as much entitled to fool around with making your own as the next guy. All you need are the following instructions, which I learned at my infamous Uncle George's knee. And it's easy, because you aren't *supposed* to be neat when you're doing this kind of job.

(My publisher told me I should leave this chapter out, because there's a chapter like it in my last book. I told him it was so interesting that it should be included here anyway.)

What you will need

Unfinished furniture is the easiest to work with, because there is no paint or varnish on it or any sealer or stain in the wood. Of course, any piece that you strip and sand down is just as good—only more work. Colonial reproductions—old, new, or in kit form—naturally are perfect.

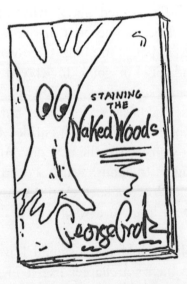

Something extra to help you in case you get hung up on staining. (Staining and Finishing Unfinished Furniture and Other Naked Woods, $1.95 *at all bookstores. Doubleday, 1968.) The book doesn't look like the picture, and the title there is just a shortcut.*

As to the finishing supplies, they make pretty good reading in themselves:

A blunt instrument, such as a lead pipe

A set of tire chains

A hammer

A sledge hammer (optional)

A shotgun filled with bird shot (A hammer and six-penny finishing nail can be substituted here.)

A clump of wet sod

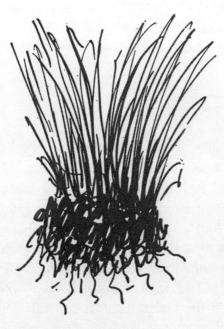

Clod of dirt with a grass handle for speeding up the aging process of your fake antiques.

1 pint of wood stain to your taste. Pine, maple, or cherry is obvious, but add half a cup of walnut to darken it. Or just use walnut, as I prefer to do. Or add something to the walnut.

A small plane or wood rasp

1 pint of shellac

3 pads of ooo-grade steel wool

1 sheet each of rough and fine production paper

A brush and rags

Newspaper for the floor

Paste wax

What you have to do

1. All sharp edges must first be rounded with the plane or wood rasp. Dig extra deep in places where wear might logically occur—on one or two corners, the tops of rungs on chairs. Then sand everything smooth with the rough and fine production paper.

2. Now beat the heck out of the piece with the chains and run them back and forth on the edges for nick marks. Get in a few good dents with the lead pipe. With the sledge hammer you can either mash a leg of a chest or smash in the side—then just push or

glue it back together again, depending on how much damage you have done.

3. For worm holes, you can fire a couple of rounds of bird shot into the piece at close range—about ten feet. Or use a sixpenny finishing nail and hammer. It will look more authentic if you group your worm holes on two legs or corners of the piece—on the sides, but not in the top. Worms go up through the legs and not often into top pieces. In real life, that is.

4. Now that you have messed the wood up plenty, it's time to get some dirt in where it will stay. For this, use a clump—or clumps—of grass with good black earth in the roots. Scrub it in hard over the whole piece. Let it dry, which shouldn't take more than fifteen minutes, and then wipe it off vigorously with rags and smooth down really rough places with the fine production paper.

5. Mix your stain and brush it on. (If you haven't been able to find a prepared wood stain, mix as directed in Chapter 15, "The Mediterranean Look," from universal tinting colors. Let the stain dry one hour in a warm, dry room.

6. Brush on a coat of shellac straight out of the can, soaking it in and wiping off the excess with a rag as you go along, working on a couple of square feet at a time. Let this coat dry for an hour and smooth the surface lightly with the ooo-grade steel wool.

7. A second coat of shellac is optional. If you decide to use a second coat, thin it with about 20 per cent denatured alcohol. Brush it on thin and fast, let it

dry two hours, and rub it down with the ooo-grade steel wool.

8. Whether one or two coats of shellac have been used, finish off with a coating of paste wax. Isn't it a humdinger?

Part IV. Tricky-Dickey
Things to Do

Quick and Easy but Smart

NO one is going to teach anybody else how to paint a *trompe l'oeil* panel or country scene by talking or writing about it. These are things you have to see done. And, besides, you might not have any talent anyway. But there are still a few things I would call "decorating" that anyone can do. Anyone who can read and follow simple directions, that is. Here they are in logical order—the order in which I happened to think of them.

17. Quick and Easy but Smart

Fake marble—Coins and things in the finish—Pasting things on—Painting old sayings on pieces—Gold-leafing for showing off—Tack-on carvings and moldings—Spattering

Fake marble

Fake-marbling is often done when someone has lost the top to a Victorian table or dresser. But can you imagine a chest of drawers that looks as if it was made of solid marble? That's the kind of thing the New York decorators do in those brownstone houses on the upper East Side. It also used to be done on fireplaces, and I don't care if you put it on your ceiling. Anyway, it's pretty easy fake marble to do, because fake marble is the kind of thing you can always wipe off and try again if you don't like the results.

The trick, of course, is in putting the characteristic nervous black streaks in with a feather. But other factors are important, too. So here's the step-by-step:

1. First, you need a good smooth, non-absorbent surface. If the wood already has a smooth coat of paint or varnish on it, coat this with one coat of shellac thinned with about 10 per cent denatured alcohol.

When it's dry, rub it down with ooo-grade steel wool, and you're ready to go.

Raw or naked wood will need three coats of shellac. Each should be allowed to dry two hours in a warm room. The first two are sanded smooth with fine production paper; the last coat, rubbed smooth with ooo-grade steel wool.

2. The base color of marble is white, but not really white, and so to a pint of white enamel add:

1 tablespoonful of mineral spirits

Raw-umber tinting color by the drop, stirring well, until you have an "off white." (No exact amount can be given, because some white enamel is whiter than others. But it will be somewhere between a quarter and a half of a teaspoonful.)

3. Brush the paint on smoothly. Use a new brush so that you are sure it is a clean one.

4. Right after this—while the paint is still very wet —dip a wing feather from a medium-sized bird such as a chicken or a duck into half a pint of flat black

Fake marble is easy to paint if you use a feather and have twitchy fingers.

paint and gently squiggle it across the wet white paint, fluttering it a little every foot or so.

If you are looking at a piece of real marble or even at a picture of same, it will be easy to duplicate anything you see. And this is the best way to keep yourself from putting in too many streaks, because it's so much fun you can easily get carried away. (In which case, wipe off the whole surface with a rag dipped in mineral spirits and start over.)

5. Once you are satisfied with your illusion, let the paint dry at least twenty-four hours in a warm room— or hurry the drying by putting the piece in direct sunlight. If you are in any doubt about the marble's being thoroughly dry, let the piece sit two or three days or a week.

6. Sprinkle talcum powder on the surface and take the gloss off the enamel with ooo-grade steel wool. Dust it off, and there you are. It isn't alcoholproof, but it sure looks like marble. Of course, you can put alcoholproof varnish over the finish—in which case, don't use the talcum powder—but the illusion won't be as great.

Coins and things in the finish

The basic idea here is that it looks as if there is a dime or a nickel lying on the top of a table, but when your victim tries to pick it up, he can't. Which may sound pretty immature, but what the heck, why not

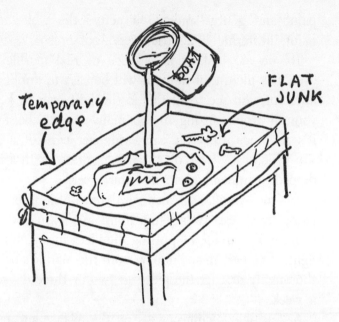

Method of applying the trick finish with things in it that your friends try to pick up and can't.

release the child within? Especially if you can make a wiseacre brother-in-law or such look silly.

For the more poetically inclined, this finish can contain fragile or colorful feathers, bugs, an old letter, ticket stub, or wedding invitation, a small photograph, stamps—just about anything that is flat.

The secret of such a thick finish—usually an eighth to a quarter of an inch thick—is that you can now quite easily buy clear liquid plastics that don't "air-dry" the way shellac, varnish, and lacquer do, but set chemically when a separate chemical hardener is mixed into them.

The most common use for liquid plastics of this kind is for applying glass cloth to the hulls of wooden boats —which greatly strengthens them, as well as making them watertight. The plastic can be machine-sanded to eggshell smoothness and finally painted.

For a tabletop or bar, you just mix in the hardener according to the directions on the can and pour it on, allowing it to level itself out. This means two things. The flat objects that you want imbedded in the plastic must first be glued down to the surface so they don't float up through the plastic. And the top must have a permanent or temporary rim around it to keep the plastic from running over the edges. (On vertical surfaces, the plastic can be brushed on only in coats of the same thickness as varnish.) A temporary edge for a top can easily be made with brown-paper tape used for wrapping parcel-post packages. After the plastic has hardened, most of the tape can be torn off and the remnants easily sanded off the edge.

Incidentally, this is a very tough, alcoholproof surface, and you don't have to do anything to it, but a coat of paste wax will keep it from scuffing or will conceal scuff marks if they develop after heavy usage.

Pasting things on

I'm not calling this section "Pasting things on" because I can't spell découpage; my reason is that découpage implies lots of little pieces of pictures of things cut out of magazines, and I think it looks awful. What I'm talking about is pasting on big pieces of things—like, for instance, wallpaper on a small chest of drawers that stands in front of a wall covered with the same paper. Very tricky.

Or, if you are mildly bohemian, you can cover a chest, cabinet, or shelves with the New York *Times* or *The Antique Trader* or *The Rural New Yorker*—or any trade newspaper that relates to your particular line or your national or ethnic background. If you're a melting-pot product, how about a piece covered, say, half with Greek and half with Irish newspapers? Tinted green. Or in the colors of the French flag, just to confuse people.

You can also use prints of paintings that fit, or can be trimmed to fit, panels on cabinet doors, staining them to look old or not staining them. The new giant-size posters of movie personalities and other personalities, which are available in any college bookstore, are also good material for those who want pop furniture.

The technique is simple. Cut the paper to the exact size. Onto the back of it brush an even coat of glue the same thickness as a coat of paint. Wallpaper paste will work, but a white glue is better. A pint should be thinned with about three tablespoonfuls of water. Apply the paper, press it tight with a pad of cotton cloth or toweling, and let it dry for at least four hours in a warm room.

The print or paper can then be tinted antique brown, pink, purple, or green with ordinary poster colors mixed in a lot of water—about three or four parts of water to one part of paint. When this is dry (overnight is best), cover it with a coat of clear spray and leave it alone. No rubbing with steel wool: instead, you can apply a coat or more of varnish over the spray coat for surfaces subject to wear. This, of course, does get rubbed down with ooo-grade steel wool and waxed.

Painting old sayings on pieces

Van Gogh and people like that used to write things all over the house. So did Eugene O'Neill. On beams, fireplaces, around the tops of chests, in heart shapes on tabletops, around the edges of tabletops—any place they felt like doing it. So why not you? Gauguin even wrote on one of his paintings—"Where do we come from? What are we? Where are we going?" In French, of course.

There are two secrets to doing it so that it doesn't come out looking as if it were written by a drunk kid. The first is to sketch the lettering or script in pencil. Pencil lines not covered by your painted letters can be erased later when the paint is dry. The second secret is that you are going to have to buy yourself an *expensive* tapered camel's-hair paintbrush in an art-supply store. Depending on the thickness of the lettering you want, this is going to run you from around $1.75 to $3.25. But these brushes are worth every penny of it. Suddenly you have talent.

Finally, the best paint to use is enamel—because of

the way it flows—and you should thin it with about a tablespoonful of mineral spirits to half a pint of enamel.

In case you can't think of anything to say, how about:

"The fault, dear Brutus, is not in our stars, but in ourselves."

"*Je t'aime beaucoup.*"

"*Viva Villa! Viva Libertad! Viva Mexico!*"

"Art is long, life short; judgment difficult, opportunity fleeting."

"*Ars longa, vita brevis, hokum aeternum est.*"

"I like Ike."

"Money won't buy poverty."

"Burn, baby, burn."

"These are the good old days—if only we knew it."

"*Voulez-vouz coucher avec moi?*"

You know, stuff like that.

Gold-leafing for showing off

This is surprisingly easy. All you do is put a thin coat of varnish on the surface you want to gold-leaf. Wait until this is almost dry—so that it is still sticky to a light touch but solid enough not to come off on your finger. Then you pick up a sheet of gold leaf with a soft, fluffy camel's-hair brush designed for the purpose, slap the gold leaf on the varnish, and gently press and stroke it smooth with a piece of fine, soft cotton or silk. If the gold leaf breaks in the application, leaving an exposed crack of varnish, just press a scrap of gold leaf over the crack, press it down, and polish it. The gold is so thin and soft that it all blends together in an astounding way.

This process is mostly used for restoring frames or completely covering small ones. But it is also used on thin decorative moldings on furniture, whether stained and varnished, or painted. In this case, the molding often is first painted vermilion (orange red). After it is dry, the vermilion is thinly varnished; when it is tacky, the gold leaf is applied. Because of the unevenness of the molding, the gold leaf is sure to crack, and the vermilion peeks through for a stunningly degenerate French effect.

Tack-on carvings and moldings

I'm sure most people think of lumberyards as places where you go to buy wood to build a house—boards, plywood, two-by-fours, and all that. But one thing I discovered in my rampant youth as a drifting odd-job man —as odd as working in a coffin factory once—was that big-city lumberyards are a horse of an entirely different color.

The reason is they don't cater to people who build houses but to interior decorators who are redoing apartments, cabinetmakers who are installing built-in hi-fi cabinets, and sweet young things who can talk their boyfriends into building bookshelves and room dividers for them.

As a result, they have wonderful assortments of hardware for sliding doors and such, a great variety of knobs for drawers, pulls for doors, plain and intricate moldings—and imitation carvings made out of pressed wood. These last include fleurs-de-lys, medallions, animals, buttons, rosettes, all in a wide range of sizes.

With these you can jazz up unfinished and lumberyard furniture, but, far more important, you can also do great things with kitchen-cabinet furniture, which is the cheapest thing you can buy in the secondhand stores. You can even use the metal cabinets, which are cheapest of all. There is not the problem of nailing the carvings onto the metal, either. They glue on with the new superstrong rubber-cement glues available in any hardware store.

Spattering

This may sound junky to you, but I've seen some lovely jobs turned out by interior decorators for rich people's houses. It's all a matter of restraint in the colors you choose and the amount of spattering you do. Consider the possibilities: a piece enameled a pale baby blue and spattered very sparingly with fine dots of white and silver; a red chest spattered with white and black; white spattered with red and black.

The trick is to thin the paint a little that you are

Spattering doesn't show dirt or wear, and it can have either a cheerful look or a sophisticated look, depending on the colors you use. This is supposed to illustrate how you spatter from the edges in.

going to spatter. Then take most of the paint off the brush by drawing it against the edge of the can. To spatter, knock the brush against the edge of a stick held in your other hand. But always start on a piece of newspaper spread on the floor next to the piece of furniture you are going to spatter. When the paint comes off the brush and makes a spot of the right size, move over to the piece. The spatter should be heaviest on risers and around the edges of flat sides and tops.

That's all. I'm going fishing.